AGAINST ALL ODDS

Release your past & Win your future!

By

Maureen A Pisani C.Ht., T.N.L.P.

Contents

Chapter 1………………….. Page 3

Chapter 2………………….. Page 5

Chapter 3………………….. Page 9

Chapter 4………………….. Page 14

Chapter 5 ………………..…. Page 16

Chapter 6………………….. Page 18

Chapter 7………………….. Page 24

Chapter 8………………….. Page 35

Chapter 9………………….. Page 50

Chapter 10…….…………….. Page 53

Chapter 11……...…………. Page 65

Chapter 12……………..…….. Page 67

Chapter 13………….……….. Page 71

Maureen A Pisani C.Ht., T.N.L.P
Maureenpisani.com

Chapter 1

I sat there smiling to myself, staring into the mirror, tears of joy streaming. Actually, I corrected myself - these were tears of accomplishment! It felt surreal, like it was not quite true, but yet I knew I had lived it. After tonight's presentation, I was an international speaker. I had been a speaker, a prolific author, and therapist for a while, but an 'International Speaker?' That happened today! And to think that a few years ago, the American medical system had declared me 100% disabled!

I remember hoping for such an opportunity in the beginning of my career. How 'maybe sometime in the future' seemed almost like I was wishing for a fairytale to come true. Yet today I remembered how the audience welcomed me. As the emcee read my introduction, even I was impressed with all the accomplishments listed. I had always taken it in stride, but put together, I had to admit to myself that it was quite a list. Their response to being introduced to me was one of respect, and even if I say so myself, admiration. This took me by surprise because I have never really felt like a "big deal." I have always been just me – 'Maureen from Malta!'

That statement always makes people stop and ask, 'From where?' when asked where I am from, because the accent is and will always be noticeable, I reply with 'Yes, the Island of Malta.'

3

This tiny jewel of an island in the center of the Mediterranean Sea that is 9 x17 miles and too small to make it onto a map is where I was born and raised.

The audience here too, was curious, so I explained briefly the highlights about the island – the amazing history, the incredible archeological sites, the phenomenal scuba diving locations and delicious food; not to mention the unparalleled hospitality of the Maltese people.

As is my usual technique when presenting, I took them through how I came to be a hypnotherapist by sharing my personal story. I could see the shock in their faces when I shared the pictures of my slashed arms. I could hear the gasps of surprise when I told them that at 32, I had been declared 100% disabled, put on Social Security, offered a lifetime supply of medication and sent away.

The presentation went much better than I expected. It landed in a way where dots connected and the audience not only understood the science I explained, they understood the effectiveness of the technique and the instant possibilities that how what I was explaining could help them too!

Now, staring at the mirror, still having this incredible experience resonate through every cell, I knew that I had not shared everything. I could not.

4

I had highlighted Malta in the best of ways. If asked, I would politely state that my childhood was chaotic.

> *How would you classify your childhood? What are the lingering effects that you still face on a regular basis? Now, looking back, what significant turning points occurred in your life that you are just becoming aware of, consciously?*

Chapter 2

I rarely spoke of my childhood or my past, but a close friend had asked me specifically why I did not talk about my past in Malta. Upon sharing some of the stories with her, she understood why I live life this way. She advised me that for people to trust me they needed to know me. From that point on, if the opportunity arose, I would share - cautiously, bits and pieces, according to the situation and discovered that the listeners always benefited from it.

Whether in professional or social settings, some people like to ask the question "What makes you – YOU?"

5

I understand that they are just asking as a conversation starter, so usually I jokingly respond with "I'm a Gemini! There's two of me! Isn't that enough?" They chuckle and the conversation flows.

The reality is that what makes me, me is a unique combination of experiences that some might not even imagine, let alone live through.

The most impactful experience in my life happened on Easter Sunday morning when I was almost 9, and my Dad had his third heart attack in one week.

Mum was at church, and my Dad woke me up, moaning, "Maureen, wake up, I'm dying...Maureen, wake up, I'm dying." As I was the oldest of three kids, the official 'BIG sister' and being a nosey-body, I had asked Mum what had been happening to Dad, especially because we had doctors coming to the house at all hours of the day and night. My mother prepared me with some instructions for the *just-in-case* situation, never realizing that I'd implement them correctly in a couple of days. Thankfully, that Sunday morning, I knew what to do and was intricately involved in saving my Dad's life.

My childhood ended that morning. I can see that now. From that point on, I never felt like a child anymore, I felt like I do right now – I am Maureen and I handle situations. That is what made me who I am!

6

In Malta, family is the foundational unit of society. Family is everything – extended family is just family to us. First cousins, second cousins, cousins once removed... they are all cousins to us. Everyone connected to us is family and family is loved and accepted... usually.

When I was around 7 years old, we were all at the summer house, a beachfront property where about half of the family lived. It was fun. The adults all lent a hand in 'parenting' the kids when appropriate, while we kids had a blast with having most of our cousins with us 24/7.

The Maltese people were conquered at least 24 times in recorded history, and as a result, there are all kinds of body shapes and hair/eye color combinations. Yes, the 'ethnic' Maltese is known to have olive skin with dark brown eyes and dark brown or black hair. That was my Dad's coloring. My mother, sister, and brother are redheads with green eyes and milky-white skin. Then, there was me. I had the olive skin, but I had blonde hair and grey eyes. My family was on the chubby side, while I was a skinny twig. The differences were obvious. I was actually mistaken for my sister's 'friend' once, instead of the automatic understanding that I was her sibling.

7

One morning, my grandma, whom I loved tremendously, wanted to talk to me. As I followed her into the living room, I ran a mental check on how naughty I had been over the last couple of days.

Back then I had a reputation of being more than mischievous. To the best of my recollection, I had not broken anything or hurt anyone, so apart from knowing that I wasn't going to be punished, I really had no idea why grandma wanted to talk to me.

She sat on the couch. I sat on the floor, cross-legged, with my arms on the seat of the couch, looking up at her. She leaned forward and spoke softly so only I heard her. The rest of the family was in the next room dealing with a late breakfast.

My grandmother took a deep breath and said "Maureen, you better study. Your sister is the beauty of the family, so you better study." I just sat there, looking at her. I thought to myself *I'm ugly*? Is that it? So I looked up at her and asked, "I'm ugly?" She did not respond. I had to check now, because I was not sure what this was all about – "Am I in trouble?" I asked. She shook her head and said "No, you're not in trouble. Off you go and have your breakfast."

I stood up from that couch feeling completely different than I had a few minutes ago. I was ugly. It was a fact.

Maureen A Pisani C.Ht., T.N.L.P
Maureenpisani.com

My grandma, whom I loved and who I felt loved me, was an adult, and so what she had said had to be true, right? It had to be. From that moment on, for about 33 more years, I had a deep knowing that echoed within me. It was the deepest foundation within me. To me it was true. Inside me, I thought of myself as - I am Maureen. I am a girl. I am ugly. There was no emotion attached to it. To me it was a fact. So, I just got on with life. I did not share it with anyone. For over three decades, that truth resonated within me. There was no need to question it – grandma loved me, right? She would not steer me wrong, would she?

Ironically, that experience did benefit me, because I did study. That conversation changed how I responded to the world. While I saw others present themselves to the world according to how they felt and looked, I worked through the years according to what I could do, what I could produce, and how I could help.

It was a liberating experience when finally, at around 40 years of age, life would truly prove to me how wrong she was. The question is, how would my life have been if I had gone through those decades without that label? Which opportunities had I grasped, and which had I missed, because of how I thought of myself?

What labels have you been given that have affected you? How do you think of yourself? How do you live your life? What labels identify you?

Chapter 3

My parents were not ready or prepared for a child like me. They wanted their children to be dainty, polite, well-behaved, obedient, and calm, but instead their first born was a ball of energy, a nightmare of a tomboy, who took exploring her world to a new level. They were constantly either admonishing me or administering first aid.

However, as mischievous as I was with cousins and classmates, I was inherently shy with outsiders.

I was authentically me with my family, friends (who were all classmates), and with my cousins; but when I was expected to be the bubbly, full-of-energy Maureen in front of strangers, I wished I could hide between the paint and the wall.

AGAINST ALL ODDS
Release your past & Win your future!

To make things more interesting, I switched three schools in three years in high school. I went from a private Catholic school, to public school, to a magnet school. Each change brought on a new group of girls. During those years, I started to stutter and stammer. It was awful. Not only was I shy, but now, when I had to speak up in class, especially during English Literature, where reading out loud was mandatory, I died a thousand deaths. Waiting for my turn was torture, and then when it was my turn, I could barely get a word out.

The teacher would sarcastically comment on how 'one sentence from Maureen was more than enough' and I would wish to become invisible.

What situations did you have to face in your teenage years? How did they affect who you became as an adult? What are you still holding onto nowadays from back then? How much better would your life be if you decided to release that baggage?

11

Maureen A Pisani C.Ht., T.N.L.P
Maureenpisani.com

For as far back as I can remember (after that infamous conversation with grandma), I had this urge. It was impossible to ignore. It's one of the things that makes me – ME! I needed to learn, I had to learn, I need to learn, I must learn... anything and everything. If there was a new experience, a new 'something' that I didn't know... I simply had to observe and learn it. I had taken it for granted that if I observed closely enough, I would learn the steps and then if, or rather when, I implemented those steps, I too, would achieve that successful result! I had utilized that process often enough to believe it to be a constant within me.

Truth be told, I really thought I could learn everything and anything. That is, until I faced my kryptonite - Organic Chemistry. I was in college learning the sciences – Physics, Biology and Chemistry.

I was an average student. If I applied myself, I knew I could improve, but there was a different reaction inside when it came to Organic Chemistry. It just did not make sense to me.

Being an extremely visual person, all I saw on the blackboard was C's, H's and O's, all jumbled up. It did not matter how much I studied; all I saw was alphabet soup.

I knew I was not going to pass. I kept it a secret. Nobody knew how stressed I was, or so I thought.

Maureen A Pisani C.Ht., T.N.L.P
Maureenpisani.com

I started having breathing issues. I could never really take in a full deep breath. That 'full lung' feeling was always elusive. I would continue dragging in the breath for as long as I could, in a desperate attempt to get that full feeling of a complete inhale. Then, to make things worse, I developed these blotches on the front of my neck that were just awful. These red blisters were about 2 inches in diameter and were ghastly. However, I still thought I had it under control. My big secret was still a secret.

Until one day, I was called to the Dean's office. My classmates were all making fun of me, snickering that the 'quiet one' was a secret troublemaker. As I followed the Dean's assistant, I scoured my brain to come up with what I could have possibly done to be called to *his* office. Nothing could have prepared me. As the assistant opened the door to the Dean's office, I saw Mum and Dad sitting at his desk! I was horrified. My first question was "Who died?"

Smiling, the Dean gently put me at ease by simply saying, "No one died, Maureen. We're here for you." For me? Really? Why? Well it turned out that my classmates had complained about my breathing issues to the teachers, who had complained to the heads of the departments, who had reported this situation to the Dean, who in turn called my parents and voila, the meeting was happening, right here, right now!

13

I was flabbergasted. I had no idea what to say, so I just sat there, looking at my hands.

The Dean took charge and started asking me all kinds of questions to see what could have possibly been going on in my life that was causing me this intensity of stress. It turned into an interrogation session, where he was just shooting questions at me. Some included "Are you being bullied?" "Are you being threatened?" "Are you being molested?"

I was mortified! After what seemed like a never-ending bombardment of questions, I finally broke down and yelled "I am failing Chemistry! There is nothing I can do! I just do not understand it! There is no way I will get an A because I am failing the class!" THERE IT WAS. MY SECRET - OUT IN THE OPEN.

There they sat and smiled. There was a collective sigh of relief. There it was - this horrible piece of information that I had just shared, and they were sighing in relief!

I did not understand it. Of course, now I understand that the truth was mild compared to what they had imagined.
What happened then was interesting. I realized that I could fail at something and still be ok. I had let down my parents in something that was completely up to me, and they were understanding.

14

What secrets are you still holding onto? How are they affecting you? How much better will you be once you have freed yourself from them? When you think of all this, do those incidents still have the same impact on you? Do they have the same value for you? Or has their effect on you depreciated with time?

Chapter 4

Growing up in Malta was not what most would expect. Most envision this idyllic island in the azure Mediterranean Sea, where everyone is happily skipping down pathways on their way to spend their entire day at the beach.

Sorry, but life in Malta is just that – Life. Malta's got all the ups and downs that everyone else experiences, and in some cases downs that most do not think about!

In Malta, I had a sickness that does not exist anywhere else – chronic appendicitis. Yes, you read it correctly!

Everywhere else on the planet, once one has had an appendix attack, it is instantly removed.

15

However, with me, from age 6 through 21, every 18-24 months I had an appendix attack, where I would be taken to the hospital, admitted, kept under observation, given an IV drip, and after a few days, sent home.

My first experience at 6 years of age was traumatic. However, as the years went by, I got accustomed to the routine of how my condition was handled there. Finally, at age 21, after being hospitalized again subsequent to another attack, the surgeon with his endless line of interns looked down his nose at me and said "Maureen, can you appreciate that you are the perfect candidate to have an appendix attack while being pregnant?" To which I answered that I did. The surgeon continued with "So what do you want to do about it?"

Really, this mighty, powerful surgeon, who had nurses and interns shaking in their boots, was asking ME what I wanted to do about it! It was almost comical. A decision which should have been made by every single surgeon who had examined me in the past 15 years was now in my hands. I looked at the surgeon and said, "I want an appendectomy now, so that scenario will never happen." The surgery was scheduled, and with that I became the first *elective* appendectomy on the books for them.

I knew I had to take control because nobody else had. In all those years, each time I was doubled over in pain, they waited. Each time, *they* risked *my* life.

16

All those professionals who had the training to make educated decisions to better their patients' health, did not. I realized that I was in charge of me. I knew it had to be done. Considering how incredibly dangerous it would have been if I had been pregnant and needed an appendectomy, it was incredibly easy for me to make that decision.

What decisions have you been forced to make? Where do you feel others, more qualified than you, could have stepped up and helped? What was the learning about yourself as you look back on that decision that you did make?! How much stronger do you know yourself to be, because of that decision?

Chapter 5

Years later I found myself working in that same hospital. St. Luke's Hospital was the only one on the island. A 1,500-bed hospital for a population of around 500,000 people. As an X-Ray Technician,

17

I loved helping patients. I enjoyed the process of having to create specific images even when the patients could not be in the required positions. The thinking outside the box approach is what I truly cherished.

One Saturday morning, I received a call from my Dad. It was extremely unusual because when on duty, calls were not allowed. However, Dad had an emergency and they put him through to me. Dad was really panicked because he thought Mum was having a stroke. He commented that her face looked like the window blinds when the cord tears.

On hearing this, I told him that I would find out who was in the Neurology Department and let him know what the next step was. I had been a patient there, so they knew me well and plus, I was staff, so I went directly to the head of the department – the top neurosurgeon for the country, whom I knew.

I explained to him what Dad had said and he replied with "Maureen, you know how the process works, I will see your mother when the schedule permits." He swiveled on a heel and walked away from me. That response, as you can imagine, was unacceptable to me.

I looked all over the place, and found that the second in charge, a phenomenal Polish neurologist, who was also an incredible gentleman, was available. I told him the exact same information and his response was "Maureen, tell your Dad to bring your mother in and I'll see her in the clinic. Just let me know when they arrive." Now, that was much better, right? I told Dad. They showed up. I let the neurologist know and he came, examined her, and even told her that he was being more thorough because I was staff!

He diagnosed Mum with Bell's Palsy, a temporary condition that, yes, resembles a stroke.

As Mum, Dad, the neurologist, and I were walking out of the clinic, the neurosurgeon walked into the hallway and caught us exiting the neurologist's office. Instantly, he knew what I had done. Everyone froze. He walked up to me, stopped about 5 inches away from my face, and lost complete control.

He screamed at me for what seemed like forever, but it had to be at least 7-10 minutes. Nobody moved. Nobody said anything.

After he had exhausted all his anger at my obvious defiance, he again swiveled on a heel and stormed out of the clinic.

We stood there for a couple of seconds and then a nurse looked at me and said, "How could you stay so calm?" I was unflappable. I hadn't reacted. I had stayed completely motionless.

"Well…." I responded, "He caught us AFTER the examination and diagnosis were completed. There was nothing he could do… and he knew that! That is why he was livid. If he had found out what I had planned before the examination had occurred, I would have had a different response." At that, the others chuckled, the stress was relieved, and Mum and Dad went back home.

I knew then and I still know now, that if there is something that needs to happen, I will make it happen. That experience taught me that sometimes the rules need to be bent for the right reasons.

What drastic action have you had to take? What rules have you bent? And… for what reasons? What was the outcome? Are you pleased with how you handled things? And if not… what will you do the next time you need to step up?

Maureen A Pisani C.Ht., T.N.L.P
Maureenpisani.com

Chapter 6

One of the things I grew up knowing about myself, deep down in my heart, was that I wanted to have children. My Dad was the 'baby whisperer.' It did not matter where we were, regardless of whether he knew the family or not, babies were drawn to him. My Dad loved babies and they knew it. Luckily, I inherited that from him. I, too, am good with babies, and I love them tremendously, too. So, imagine the heartbreak when I found out I could not have any children.

I had grown up with the traditional hopes of the 'happily ever after' future, longing to go through life checking the appropriate boxes, but apparently it was not meant for me.

One day I was 'normal,' and then at 26, I ended up having emergency surgery on December 22nd to remove two huge masses. These endometriomas were 6cm and 11cm in diameter, which automatically came with a diagnosis of Stage IV Endometriosis.

To make a long story short, after a couple of surgeries it was determined that there was no way, physically, that I could conceive naturally. I felt like the rug had been pulled from beneath my feet. How could I, of all people, ME not be able to have children? I was ready! I had done everything by the book! I had followed all the guidelines and directions! I had been a good girl! I was a good wife! Why me??????

21

I was shocked, and actually I was even embarrassed about it. I felt like I was letting my husband down, and I felt less-than all other women, especially the ones who complained that they got pregnant too fast! I was envious of every lady that proudly showed off her baby-bump.

I took it hard. I could not talk it out with anyone, not even my husband. He already blamed me for all this inconvenience,

I knew he did not have compassion about this. He was ready for children, and it was my job to produce children. Only my body was not complying.

We ventured into the fertility world. After more tests and more surgeries, the specialists recommended In-Vitro Fertilization (IVF) as a solution for us to have children of our own.

The good girl in me had to come to a decision. The Catholic Church at the time was adamantly against IVF, but I wanted to have children, and this was the only way I could possibly succeed. I debated for a while, but the internal biological clock won.

I had really hoped to never have to go against what Church doctrine stated, but this was the rest of my life! This was my marriage!

Maureen A Pisani C.Ht., T.N.L.P
Maureenpisani.com

After a while, I acquiesced, and the IVF treatments began. Step by step, I went through it all. The woman who hated needles got 2 shots a day for 5 weeks. It was not fun. Then, thankfully, the process worked, and we ended up with 6 embryos. I was elated!

The husband decided he did not want multiples, that one baby was more than enough, so three embryos were implanted. The feeling of carrying three new souls within me, was MONUMENTAL! Imagine being trusted with a one-of-a-kind treasure, imagine how overly cautious you would be in how you handled it and how you took care of it. Yes, that is exactly how I felt! I did everything by the book. I was the model patient.

Then one day, the world stopped for me. I was at work, happy, going through my day, when suddenly I felt a warm 'whoosh' feeling in my pelvis. It was the worst feeling possible.

In my heart I knew that it was the beginning of the end. A few hours later, I miscarried the triplets. It did not matter how much my heart and soul wanted to hold onto them. God had decided. Nature had decided. It was done. They had come, shown up in my life, transformed me, and left. It was completely out of my control. I was never the same. I understood loss so much more.

23

All I know is that the moment the realization hit, I wished I were dead. I had let everyone down. God had entrusted me with three souls, and I had miscarried them.

All the fingers were pointing at me. I, Maureen, had let God down. To say that I was devastated would be an understatement. I cried inconsolably, for hours. The loss was gargantuan, I have no words to describe it. There was no explanation.

According to the specialists, I fell into the inexplicable 10% – the unwarranted spontaneous abortion that happens when the body decides to expel the baby or in my case, babies.

I was devastated. I was broken, sad, depressed, in mourning for the death of my children, embarrassed, confused, and lost. It just did not make sense to me. I had done everything exactly how I was supposed to but... unforeseen tragedy still happened. I was inconsolable. How was I supposed to go on after this? I wanted to die. I knew I would not commit suicide, so I prayed for God to call me home. He did not. Every breath I inhaled felt like my body was betraying me over and over. I did not want to breathe, I wanted to be dead, like my children.

Maureen A Pisani C.Ht., T.N.L.P
Maureenpisani.com

My friends heard about what happened, but nobody reached out. What could they say? What words of comfort could they offer me? There were none that would help.

I knew that and didn't even expect their calls. I had nothing to say either.

All I had was tears. I ran the scenario through my head thousands of times a day. I searched through my memories, what had I done wrong? Where had I triggered this tragedy? Then I found it! A few days before it happened, I had been so happy that I skipped a few steps as I was walking from home to the car. It couldn't have been that, could it? Did that skipping dislodge something?

On my next appointment, I asked the doctor. With kind smiling eyes, he gently shook his head and stated that skipping did not cause the miscarriage. He looked me straight in the eyes and said, "Nature sometimes takes a pre-emptive blow to what we consider to be perfect."

There were endless months of crying. I could not walk past a stroller without tearing up. I could not walk past babies of different ages, without instantaneously comparing the baby with how mine would have looked. I learned what a hypocrite was, each time I forced myself to wish someone congratulations on their pregnancy.

25

It was tough. Especially when I returned to work weeks later, only to find out that the COO of the company had demoted me from Dispatch Manager to Receptionist because I 'was not my usual self' on my return!

Looking back, I have insights as to why all that happened.

Seven months after the miscarriage, after refusing to participate in behavior that went against my ethics, morals, and beliefs, I was thrown out of my own home. Four months after that he told me he wanted a divorce.

At 28, I was alone, divorced, mourning miscarried triplets, living in a furnished studio apartment, because all I had taken with me were clothes and books. I was facing a new future which was the epitome of unchartered waters.

Nothing in my past had prepared me for this outcome. I had no idea what to do.

> *What tragedy have you faced? How did it affect you? How have you dealt with it? What have you learned from it? What attributes and strengths did those crises uncover for you?*

Chapter 7

I realized that there was one thing I could do: I took one day at a time. Talk about being a cliché! I went to work and returned home. I went grocery shopping and went home. End of story. That was all that was required of me to pretend that I was doing well.

Once I was home, all the emotions that I had pushed down deep inside me, during the day came out. If I needed to cry, I did, until I ran out of tears. If I needed to yell, I did, until I lost my voice. The only way to go past it was to go through it, so I did.

Once home, safe in my studio apartment, I did not have to pretend to be professional or polished or in control.

There in that tiny room I could be completely uncensored, unpolished, raw, vulnerable, broken, in pain, sobbing my heart out. I could be me. And I was.

I was raised in a society where a marriage was lifelong. I was raised to expect that the man who vowed in front of the family, the community, and God, to stand by me, did. I had seen MEN who had honored that promise made to their wives in front of God.

Maureen A Pisani C.Ht., T.N.L.P
Maureenpisani.com

I was raised to believe that marriages led to families and in turn to happy futures. None of that happened for me. I now believed that I had done something horrible and this was my punishment.

Three months into this new chapter, I stepped out of the building into the parking lot. It was late December, early in the morning. I had a moment of enlightenment. It hit me – I had NOT done anything wrong! I had been the example of a good wife! I WAS ethical AND honorable! There was NOTHING for me to feel guilty about!

I remember standing right there on that step, having all these thoughts run through my head when an excited utterance escaped my lips stating,

"Why the hell am *I* feeling guilty?" And that was that. I was over it. I was over all the guilt of the broken marriage. My heart was still broken about the loss of the children, but that was a wound I knew would take a much longer time than a few months.

Life continued, home to work, work to home. Slowly, gradually I started shifting into this calm routine. There were topics that were too sensitive to broach in public, but for the most part, I was surviving.

Maureen A Pisani C.Ht., T.N.L.P
Maureenpisani.com

Changes happened. I changed jobs, moved to a new apartment, bought my own stuff, and created a new home. I was stable. I was happy in my little world. I was coming to terms that my life was not going to fall within the 'average' category.

I was learning to be a single lady in America. It was all brand new to me. I was astonished with the advice my colleagues gave me with regard to what behavior was acceptable and what was not. I heard all their advice, thanked them, and went home.

In these times of massive change, I have always found that limiting the distractions in my life always worked for me.

I imagined how I would feel if I did go out and date! That would mean postponing the receiving of all the understandings I needed to learn. So… NO. Staying home, letting my mind process what had happened, letting my heart catch up with all that had happened, and starting the healing process from the ultimate of betrayals was what needed to happen.

I had gone from my parents' house to my married home, and then to being completely alone in America. My entire family was all in Malta. I needed a little more time to acclimate to my new surroundings. I needed to get to know who I was. Who had I become?

Maureen A Pisani C.Ht., T.N.L.P
Maureenpisani.com

I can tell you at that stage I was beyond bitter and scarred. I remember publicly offering a colleague my condolences on her engagement announcement. I chuckle now, but I remember truly meaning how sorry I felt for her nuptial journey.

I decided that my next chapter should be learning something new. At that time, I was a Medical Historian for a medical group comprised of three orthopedic surgeons. I took the patients' histories so the doctors could read their entire background in a concise and efficient manner.

Considering that I have always enjoyed helping patients, typed at the speed of speech, and knew medical terminology, I took to this job like a duck to water. I was meeting interesting people, and as luck would have it, I found the perfect opportunity to learn Spanish! In a few months, I was able to take an entire patient history in Spanish! I was having fun and helping patients. I liked it!

However, after about 18 months of long hours of typing at the speed of speech, my arms started to bother me. In the beginning it was the occasional ache in one forearm. Then it was every evening after work. Then it was both forearms aching all day long. Then it worsened to where the elbows hurt. When I started dropping things, I knew that my grip strength was weakening. It was time to speak up.

The doctors had a nerve conduction study done on my arms, which determined that there was intense nerve damage. They recommended surgery. I had worked with these doctors, and I trusted them, so I agreed to the surgeries.

When the pain in the first arm to be operated on – the right arm, did not diminish after the first surgery, their comment was "Oh no! It couldn't have been the wrong spot, could it?"

We did the second and third surgeries on the right arm, always hoping that things would improve. They did not.

You know how there are moments in time that are etched in your brain? They are 'stills' in the movie of your life. It was the day of the second surgery on the right arm. I was in the surgery center, prepped, lying on a gurney which was parked on the side of the wall right before the OR door. All the staff was busy going somewhere or doing something. I felt completely invisible. They talked to each other, walked with a purpose and not one of the staff looked at me. It was quite disheartening. Then the anesthesiologist came over.

A brusque man of few words, he barely introduced himself. He grabbed my left forearm and without warning jabbed this huge needle into the side of the forearm. He was so rough, and it was so painful, that I broke out in a cold sweat! He looked at the intravenous cannula, shook his head, muttered under his breath "Well that won't do," yanked it out of my arm, and walked away. There I was – surrounded by busy staff, while my arm was bleeding onto the sheets. I remember thinking that I was going to bleed to death.

I have to say that that was one of the few moments in life where I felt that nobody cared about me. I had already been fearful of needles. That experience got me to the point where I was terrified of them.

I ended up in an unfortunate predicament, where the right arm was incredibly painful because it was recuperating from three surgeries done in the space of a few months. The left arm was also incredibly painful because the nerve damage had been aggravated due to overcompensation, because I could barely use my right arm and so the left had to work more. I was miserable. As I write this, I find myself cringing as I remember those horrible days. The pain was constant. Any movement just intensified and aggravated the arms. The pain pills did nothing, but I took them anyway because the thought of having more intense pain than what I was currently experiencing was terrifying.

We came to the point where the doctors recommended operating on the left elbow. By now my fear of needles had escalated tremendously, so I asked the surgeons if they would perform all three procedures on the same day. They agreed.

[Please, NEVER ask for multiple procedures to be done on the same day. By the time the third site was operated on, the joint was so swollen and distorted, I have no idea what they did.]

Once I had been in recovery for their official time of recuperation, I was sent home still very groggy, not really knowing what to expect. What followed three surgeries on one joint on the same day was nothing short of hell on earth. The intensity of the pain was indescribable.

The left arm hurt. I mean, way more than the right arm did. Something was wrong. The surgery had been done on a Friday, so over the weekend, the throbbing, searing pain had increased to a point where I could not lay the arm down on anything. I remembered the intensity of the post-surgical pain on the right arm, but this was much worse.

Any movement would send shooting pain from my elbow down to my fingertips and up to my skull. It felt like I was being whipped.

Monday morning, I called the office requesting an emergency appointment with the doctor who had done the surgeries. Please keep in mind that I was still an employee of that Medical Group at this time.

The first thing I heard the surgeon say to the nurse through the phone was for me to settle down and get over it. According to him, this was regular post-surgical pain and I should know by now what to expect. I reiterated to the nurse, that this was different.

This pain was much more intense and unrelenting. Again, he invalidated my statements.

I kept fighting to go in and get it checked. I KNEW that something was wrong.

Not to seem too uncaring, to everyone around him, the surgeon finally acquiesced for me to go in. I lived less than 10 minutes away so as soon as I could get myself semi-presentable, I made arrangements to be driven there. I walked in and sat in the waiting room.

I was an employee of the group. Maybe I was slightly selfish, but I really did expect them to call me in ASAP! That unfortunately did not happen.

The patients who were in the waiting room were all seen and released.

Maureen A Pisani C.Ht., T.N.L.P
Maureenpisani.com

Other patients came in and were seen before me. I was left sitting there in the waiting room until I was the last patient of the day.

I had had three procedures done on Friday by my own boss, who, because I had not submitted to his rhetoric, made me wait until he had seen every other patient before having the staff call me in.

My colleagues could barely look me in the face. I was taken in and the cast and the bandages were removed. The last layer of wadding was left so he could remove it carefully.

When the surgeon peeled off that last layer, there were two huge blisters bloated with blood.

One was about 1½ inches, while the other was longer than 2 inches. I just stared at him. He had the decency to pause. He took a breath in and stated, "Well, you must be much more sensitive than I thought. He gave orders on how my left elbow was to be treated and walked out. Never did he apologize or acknowledge that I had been correct in stating that something was wrong. I sat there, tears of fury and indignation streaming down my face. I have never been more furious with anyone in my life. How dare he? How dare he ridicule my complaints?

35

How dare he decide what was happening without examining me? How dare he attempt to invalidate what I was feeling!

I knew something was wrong and I had continued pushing for what I knew was the correct way to handle it. It turned out I had been right. I had spoken up and stood my ground for the right thing to be done!

What incident still riles you up? Who do you remember invalidating your opinion? How did you handle it? How would you have liked to have handled it? What lesson did you learn about that individual? What lesson did you learn about yourself?

After each procedure on the right arm, the cast had stayed on for three weeks. When I went for one of my regular follow-up appointments, the surgeon wanted to remove the cast on the left arm, also after 3 weeks.

I asked him if that was appropriate, considering that the elbow had had three procedures, not one.

Maureen A Pisani C.Ht., T.N.L.P
Maureenpisani.com

He looked at me and squealed, "You question me???!?!?!??" and then said to the nurse, "I will see her on my return." Little did I know that he was off to a 5-week African safari. When I returned to see him 5 weeks later, and they removed the cast, the left elbow was locked due to the excessive scar tissue build up.

After all these surgeries, I found myself in a predicament where I was losing no matter what decision I made.

Now, with both elbows operated on, I was in worse shape than before. I had lost 80% grip strength on the right and 75% on the left. The scars were gruesome. People would stop walking and just stare at my arms. One time, I was in a waiting room, when a lady across the room, in a different language which I understood, told her relative "Look at how they slashed her arms!" I was mortified.

I asked around and found an arm specialist who was willing to see me for a consult. He seemed to know what had happened and knew what to do. I agreed to have him treat me, so I switched doctors.

The first thing this new surgeon had to do was get my left elbow to move. That had to be done by the physical therapists breaking up the scar tissue.

Everyone in the treatment room would hear the crunching pops when, with sheer strength, their thumbs would break through the scar tissue. Yes, it was painful, but it was the only way to get the left elbow to be functional again.

This new surgeon also had to re-do one of the prior surgeries – a medial epicondylectomy - on both sides, because when the prior surgeon had shaved off the epicondyle, he did not shave off enough bone.

The new surgeon also did a neuroplasty, which resulted in 5-inch scars down the length of both forearms.

On the left forearm, the neuroplasty revealed a thick band of fibers that was pressing down on all the muscles and nerves. You do not have it. I should not have had it, but I did. So, it was removed. On the right forearm, the radial nerve was stuck to the supinator muscle, so the surgeon cut the muscle lengthwise and now the nerve slides in between the two halves.

Yes, each procedure meant being in a cast for weeks on end. Physical therapy followed, and of course throughout the entire time, pain pills were prescribed and swallowed. It was awful. More and more pain. Non-stop pain. Pain – morning, noon, and night. It was brutal.

Maureen A Pisani C.Ht., T.N.L.P
Maureenpisani.com

In spite of all his good intentions, the second surgeon could not understand why the pain was unrelenting. He had taken care of the physical/mechanical mishaps, and the surgical sites looked like they were healing, but the pain persisted. After endless hours of physical therapy and acupuncture, the doctor and the second medical group determined that we had reached the end of the line.

After 6 years of hell.... the medical conclusion was to have the system declare me 100% disabled, put me on Social Security, offer me a lifetime supply of medication and wash their hands of me. And I was only 32!

I was furious! What? Disabled? Social Security? Are you kidding me? I did not come to the best country on the planet to be labelled 'disabled!' I was livid.

My reaction took them by surprise! So much so that they sent me to several psychiatrists to see why I was so upset! Seriously. I cannot make this up.

Each of the specialists would question me as to why I thought I could have a productive future.

Maureen A Pisani C.Ht., T.N.L.P
Maureenpisani.com

I remember one time I was literally pointing my finger at the psychiatrist's face, loudly stating 'Just you wait and see. I'll make something of myself." And he responded with "Oh really? What are you going to do?" And that was the glitch. I had no idea.

I remember spending hours sitting on the couch, staring a black TV (because I did not even have the stamina to turn it on), praying to God, actually begging God "Please God, give me a life. Please God, give me a life."

When have you faced a dark valley in life? How did you go through it? What did you learn once you emerged from it? What did hindsight offer you as hidden blessings? As you look back, how much stronger do you find yourself to be today?

Maureen A Pisani C.Ht., T.N.L.P
Maureenpisani.com

Chapter 8

During this time, I had been dating this single dad who was raising his three kids, ages 16, 19, and 21 at the time. It felt like they were a jigsaw puzzle missing a piece, and that piece was me. Again, I found myself in unchartered territories because I wanted to be there for them, but I did not want them to feel like they were betraying their mother. I promised them my honesty, my confidentiality, and my support. I kept that promise until the end.

The family dynamics were the Dad and the three kids, as a unit, and then if it suited everyone – me. In the beginning I totally understood that this was to be expected. But after 10 years, when they called family meetings, I was still asked to take the dog for a long walk.

I cannot tell you why that happened, because during those 10 years, I gave them my best. I know I came from a different culture, but I did help, support, teach, give generously, and love each one of them.

I realize that I'm only responsible for my actions. I know I gave them my best. As much as I wanted it to be a happy family, I was never let 'in.'

Maureen A Pisani C.Ht., T.N.L.P
Maureenpisani.com

Over the years, there's a piece of me that I jokingly call "Maureen from Malta," and that piece feels like it has just come off the boat last night. That piece of me, even decades later, will always be the foreigner and is tickled pink with 'Americana.'

As luck would have it, there was going to be a Chamber of Commerce fair close by where I lived at the time, where the car from the 70's TV show 'Starsky & Hutch' was going to be on display. Of course, I simply HAD to go see it!

There I was, the only one visibly excited that the car – the one I had seen on TV in my childhood – was right there in front of me. That morning is permanently etched into my brain. That day was pivotal.

As I was walking around, scanning the other booths, there was a lady offering a Free Handwriting Analysis. Considering that I was on Social Security at the time, that was all I could afford – Free.

I gave her a handwriting sample… and…she read me like a book! I was astonished! I asked how and where she had learned it.

Maureen A Pisani C.Ht., T.N.L.P
Maureenpisani.com

This prim and proper Asian lady, the epitome of grace and elegance, looked over to her right and then to her left, and then without any fanfare, slid a brochure towards me, stating, "Call them." That was it. There was no pitch, no hype, no close. Done. Call them, she said, and I did.

The next day, I went in for my interview to learn about this mysterious topic called 'Hypnosis.' I had no idea what it was. I had two questions for the Director who interviewed me. He was a kind gentleman, who, when I asked, "Does any of this go against the Church?" smiled and promised that everything taught at that college was scientific, which it was. Then, risking all hope I asked, "Can you do this without your arms?"

He paused, looked down at the raw, angry, glaring scars on my forearms, looked up and said, "If you can snap your fingers, you can." It was the moment of truth. I looked at my right (dominant) hand, the one with the greater loss of strength, and gave it my all. AND…. I was successful! I could snap my fingers!

The beginning of the journey was simultaneously exhilarating and excruciating! I loved learning. My mind was absorbing everything, but my arms complained tremendously.

43

The drive to the college, even though only 8 miles, was playing havoc with my arms. A few weeks into it, I went to the Director and shared that the pain was truly interfering with my ability to learn. He suggested that maybe a hypnotherapy appointment might help.

I chose one of the senior faculty members who had been mentored by the late founder of the college.

I went in for my first appointment with nothing to lose (because I felt I had already lost everything).

The hypnotherapist, an older gentleman, was almost flippant about this arm pain situation that was hindering my learning. He asked me endless questions, and I answered. At one point, he started the hypnotic portion. To tell you the truth, it was anticlimactic. I did not feel a thing. I felt like I was wide awake, I did not feel any tingling, or magic, or…anything! AND I was definitely NOT asleep! I walked out of that office befuddled.

However, the next morning, the pain from the shoulders to the wrists had disappeared! I only had pain in the hands. The next week, I went in for my second appointment and again, he asked more questions, I gave more answers, he hypnotized me again, and again, I still felt absolutely nothing. The next morning, there was no pain. Yes, that is God's truth!

Maureen A Pisani C.Ht., T.N.L.P
Maureenpisani.com

Six years of constant pain, ten surgeries, and over 25,000 pills, and with two sessions of hypnotherapy the pain was resolved! Do you think I believe in hypnotherapy? You better believe it! The question people ask me is the $64 million-dollar question – *"What do you think would have happened if you had had hypnotherapy FIRST?"*

As soon as my arms came back, I had a new future. I was unstoppable. I have always loved learning, and now I was learning a modality that gave tremendous results! There was a minor hiccup, however, because I was still incredibly shy. I would almost never speak up because I was extremely conscious of my accent. The hypnotherapy college thankfully, was filled with students from all corners of the world, so accents were common.

I remember one time, as the class was prepping for a test, the instructor asked a question on medical hypnosis. There were 75 students in that class, but nobody responded. The instructor demanded that someone give her an answer, and because nobody had spoken up, I did. I gave her the answer, which was correct, but as soon as I finished reciting it, someone from the back groaned "oh my gosh... she just said it word for word."

45

I had not shared with anyone that I have a photographic memory, so for me, I was reading the response from my mind's eye. That was the only time I had spoken up in class. I was so shy, that other students had forgotten I was there.

Yet, toward the end of the year training, a few ladies with whom I had become friends, shared that I had been voted "most likely to succeed" by the rest of the class! I was completely taken by surprise! Really? ME???

That's when my second future launched. Three weeks after graduating, the college offered me a position as a tutor in their online distance program.

Three months into that I was hired as the Director of Admissions for that college. It was exhilarating!

As part of my responsibilities as a Director of Admissions, I assisted the instructors with the new classes. It was a great bonding experience with the students, which ensured higher retention rates. One night, the instructor, an amazingly professional, elegant, and knowledgeable lady who was also my mentor, started sneezing while teaching class.

Suddenly, she sneezed rather harshly, clasped her right hand over her face, and waved for me to come to her with her left. Of course, I ran up and she whispered "I am having a nosebleed. Take over." and ran out of the class. I looked at her notes and noticed that the next item on her schedule was a demonstration.

I realized that none of these students had ever seen this kind of technique, so I chose a volunteer and proceeded to do the demo. The process went superbly well. The young lady I had chosen responded beautifully. I was so focused on what I was doing, that when I was bringing the young lady out of hypnosis, the class started to applaud, and I jumped! Completely startled! That just made everybody chuckle. As I looked up, the instructor was in the back of the room, beaming with pride and joy at how well it had all turned out.

A couple of weeks later, while working in my office, two instructors came to my doorway. One said "Maureen, John is sick with food poisoning. Would you like to teach his class tonight?" I responded with "Yes, of course I would!" They smiled.

Then my next question was "By the way, what was he going to teach tonight?" They laughed out loud. The other instructor, also John, said to the first John, "Trust her to respond like this!"

Maureen A Pisani C.Ht., T.N.L.P
Maureenpisani.com

Teaching that first class was terrifying and terrific and addictive all at once. I loved and still love that feeling of teaching adults who are eager to learn. I remember doing live demos where volunteers would have a complementary session because they agreed to be a teaching exercise for the students. It was exhilarating to me, because the unpredictability of the session kept me on my toes and the students learned how to be flexible in their approach to clients' presenting complaints.

I was living a good life. I was the Director of Admissions, an instructor, and a mentor at one of the most prestigious accredited colleges for Hypnotherapy in the country. I was also running a full practice.

However, life at home was just passable. The husband had decided to quit his job, so I was supporting the household. I was alright with that because he said he needed a break, and he eventually decided to learn hypnotherapy too.

I was more than agreeable with his decision to become a hypnotherapist. I hoped that it would open up new worlds to him, too. However, what I had not expected was how unprofessional and underhanded the husband would turn out to be.

Maureen A Pisani C.Ht., T.N.L.P
Maureenpisani.com

Once, I was in the middle of a discussion with a lady at a store, where the conversation had turned to how I could help her navigate through a situation as her therapist. I made her an offer and was waiting for her response to book an appointment, when he, in that moment of silence, popped up and said he would see her himself for a lower price! I was shocked and livid! How dare he! I could not believe his nerve!

Of course, I stayed quiet. After all, we were in public. As soon as we were home, however, I did let him know how unbelievably unprofessional that was. I also stated that that was the one and only time he would do that to me. If he wanted clients, he had to do the work himself – go out there and network for his own practice, not swoop in on my potential clients.

A few weeks later, we were at a restaurant having lunch with the family, when the son's wife asked me if I would be willing to help her uncle stop smoking. Of course, I was happy to help. As I was giving her the terms I would give to her uncle, because he was *her* uncle, the then-husband did it again! He told her that he would work with her uncle at an even cheaper price than what I had offered her! The table went quiet. It seemed that everyone knew that what had happened was wrong on so many levels, except him!

Maureen A Pisani C.Ht., T.N.L.P
Maureenpisani.com

I shut down. I have a personal habit, that if I cannot guarantee that I am going to be polite and professional, I will not speak. I did not speak for the rest of the meal. I did not speak on the drive home. It was only when he was ready to go run some errands, did he realize that I was not talking to him. He then came at me and verbally accused me of neglecting him, and that is when I spoke up. I told him in no uncertain terms how I was done with his undermining my every move to improve. Yes, I was upset. Yes, I was mad... but I was not expecting his response. He came so close to my face that I could feel the impact of the air as he spewed out all the emotions, he had been holding in.

He screamed how much he hated how smart I was. He screamed how he hated *this* and *that* about me, how he **hated me...** on and on he went, he just kept spewing hatred and profanity.

I stood there quiet. There was nothing for me to say. However, a decision was made. That day was the day I knew that the marriage would not last.

That day I knew I would divorce him. That day, I knew that what I was experiencing was absolutely NOT love.

Maureen A Pisani C.Ht., T.N.L.P
Maureenpisani.com

Life continued. He never apologized. I never brought it up. However, the clock was ticking. Because he had not experienced any repercussions, he thought everything was fine. He kept getting bolder with his outrageous demands. Suffice to say that in 10 years, he had never allowed me to have coffee with a girlfriend. Yes, you read it correctly.

To see who I am today, makes that sentence incomprehensible. However, at the time, I was living the role of a 'dutiful wife.' I was sorely mistaken, because a 'dutiful husband' would never impose such limitations. I tolerated so much abuse for the sake of giving the marriage a chance.

By this time, the kids had all moved out and were living their own lives. The relationship had become constricted. He, the husband, had become increasingly controlling, limiting me to what I could wear, who I could talk to, and where I could go with his permission and within his imposed limits! And because I did not wish to be the one who broke up the marriage, I tolerated it all.

Until one morning, when I received a call from a former colleague whom I had not heard from for a while. He had been working in San Diego as the Financial Director at a Holistic College.

51

He had had lunch with the Dean of the college the day before and they were brainstorming on how to enhance the college and what it offered. My friend had mentioned the possibility of adding Hypnotherapy to the curriculum. The Dean liked that idea, and after evaluating several prospective applicants, they both realized that I was the perfect candidate for the Program Director Position to launch the Hypnotherapy Department. My friend's words to me on the phone were "Whatever curriculum you want to teach, whatever salary you request, whatever hours you want to work... we want YOU."

As you can imagine, I was beyond excited. I could barely believe my ears. This was an opportunity of a lifetime.

I was pacing the den when the husband finally woke up. He knew something was up, and he was not a happy man. After making sure that the first cup of coffee was done, I approached him with the news. He sat on the couch listening. After I had told him the entire offer, he asked "Where is this college?" For a man who was afraid to drive freeways, I knew this was going to be difficult. I responded with "It's in San Diego." I remember how he responded, like it was yesterday. He turned his head away, and haughtily stated "MY wife won't go there."

I was stunned, but I did not respond. Excuse me!!! What?!?!?! Are you serious??? As my head was asking all these questions, my mind came up with a definitive response. *Then, get yourself another wife!* That was the final straw of the marriage. How dare he! This was simply intolerable, and I was done.

However, one does not leave a marriage on a whim. I had to think about things.

Considering everything else I had endured; I took four additional weeks. I had to organize my thoughts. All my colleagues knew him. I was troubled by how they would take it. They didn't know the extent of how ridiculously controlling he was. How emotionally and verbally abusive he was. They could possibly judge me unfavorably.

However, it had come to the point, where even if every single colleague shunned me for my decision, I knew I still had to leave for my own sake. This had gone too far. I deserved to be happy. I knew I deserved a heck of a lot more, but happy was the most basic for me.

On a Friday afternoon, four weeks after his ultimatum, I handed him a four-page letter explaining why I could not be his wife any longer. He read it, ripped it up, and threw it in my face. He accused me of everything under the sun. He cried. He sobbed. He completely lost control.

Maureen A Pisani C.Ht., T.N.L.P
Maureenpisani.com

He shrieked - crying and yelling at the same time demanding to know how many men I had cheated on him with. My truthful reply was "None." I have always honored my vows. The drama escalated. He called all his family, still completely out of control, each time recounting the entire scenario.

I was disappointed and repulsed by his behavior. Here he was, the one who had attempted to control my every move, now completely out of control. I had to leave and leave fast. I went looking at apartments on Friday, found one on Saturday and applied for it. On Monday I was approved.

I asked a colleague whose boyfriend was a mover, if I could book him for Wednesday, and I did. Requested a day off for Wednesday and I was done.

Returning to the house was a nightmare. I truly expected him to behave with a little more self-respect. It was awful. Those last few days were sad. He tried to promise that he would change his behavior, but I had already seen his true colors and knew what his true feelings towards me were. There was no turning back. The decision had been made. He had hated me but had been comfortable usurping me and everything I brought to the table for ten whole years. Enough was enough. Nothing he could say would change my mind. I knew what the true version of him was, and I was done.

54

On Wednesday, the movers came, and I moved out in 60 minutes. It was the fastest liberation ever! These three men helped me with my stuff, and I am so incredibly grateful for their professionalism and efficiency.

Moving into a new apartment, was a new beginning on many levels for me. Especially, when I gained control of my environment. I created my little sanctuary so coming home was pleasant again. Being at home was peaceful. I could start AND finish a day in peace and calmness. I had not had *that* for a long time.

There were surprise blessings along the way. Yes, the news spread around the college like wildfire. However, one by one, each and every colleague came privately to me, offering me their support.

It was truly a blessing I had not expected to be given yet received it with an open heart. Things were looking bright. I was free.

There was such a shift of energy within me and around me that it took me by surprise. I was beyond happy, my body felt lighter and life was really good!

Maureen A Pisani C.Ht., T.N.L.P
Maureenpisani.com

I had to start re-assessing who Maureen was. I saw how people responded to me. I was cautious when stating that I had been married twice and divorced twice, because I had no idea how others would respond to that. Interestingly enough, I found out that the heaviness of the stigma was *my* doing! People generally did not care. I learned to say "Oh, I'm divorced." That was the truth, was it not? Months into my being single, enjoying the coziness of my new home, some friends insisted that I expand my social circle. We all went dancing, which I found I enjoyed thoroughly.

There was one evening I will never forget. A group of us ladies, all different ages, all different sizes, all different styles, had gone to this new club. It had a large dance floor and the venue itself was huge. I was just being me. I had gone there to dance, nothing else... but then something happened. As one guy was walking me back from the dance floor to our table, there was a line of men just standing there. I asked one of my friends what the men were doing there and her comment was "Well, they're waiting in line to dance with YOU!" Oh, my goodness! Talk about being surprised!

Since I always like to come from a factual point of view, I can now share that my grandmother's comment ceased affecting me that night.

I was able to shed that horrible comment 33 years after she had cloaked me with it. One guy saying nice things to impress me I could easily dismiss, but a whole line of men waiting to dance with me... well... facts were facts, right? And just like that, I started noticing who Maureen truly was.

However, as I started getting into my own, energy, strength, awareness, being... call it what you will, I found out the hard way that not everyone was happy for me. There was another instructor, at the college, who periodically would lash out at me. The first time occurred after I had taught a class and shared a discount for a workshop, I was teaching with the students that, to my knowledge, was beyond acceptable. He wanted to make a point that I was wrong. While in the student center, during break time, where hundreds of students were walking about, he decided to let me know what was wrong with me. We stood there facing each other. He was usually a very pale, white man, but on that evening, he was tomato red. He was standing a few inches away from me, with his right index finger about 2 inches from my cheek yelling at the top of his lungs "Do you know what's wrong with you, Maureen?"

In my head I responded, 'I think you're about to tell me' and he continued with **"YOU ARE UNSTOPPABLE!** *That's* **what's wrong with you! YOU ARE UNSTOPPABLE!"**

Maureen A Pisani C.Ht., T.N.L.P
Maureenpisani.com

In my head, all I heard was *'Don't smirk. Don't laugh because he'll have a stroke right here, right now.'* I just looked at him.

Because seriously, that is my problem? Are you kidding? To me, that's the best compliment I have ever received! I wear that attribute like a badge, with honor!

Unfortunately, even after the Dean of the college got involved, this instructor would still periodically attack me verbally, screaming in public, with witnesses present who corroborated my version of the events. Almost everyone was aware that I had not provoked him in any way. Yet for some unknown reason, my direct supervisors never took a stand against him to protect me. One day, a few weeks after I had left the college, my former director called me. His opening salutation was "I am truly sorry." Of course, that intrigued me. Apparently, that morning, that same instructor, had walked into the director's office and let loose on him – yelling and screaming at him, like he used to do with me.

Once he was done, he simply turned and walked away. The director's comment to me was that he looked at another colleague and said, "Now we know what Maureen was talking about!"

Maureen A Pisani C.Ht., T.N.L.P
Maureenpisani.com

AGAINST ALL ODDS
Release your past & Win your future!

I asked my mentor why this instructor had such an explosive reaction toward me, because it just did not make sense. Her response was that he had set some fictitious standard to where *he* thought it was appropriate for me to rise, and I'd had the gall to surpass it! Yes, can you believe it?!?!? It was preposterous!

How did your 'shining brighter' affect your work? Your life? How did you believing in yourself change how you feel? How did you prioritizing yourself upgrade your life? Did it hold you back? Did it motivate you to keep striving – onward and upward?

Maureen A Pisani C.Ht., T.N.L.P
Maureenpisani.com

Chapter 9

Life in San Diego was good. I was working as a Program Director and I loved it. I worked a full day – two 5-hour lectures a day and running the department during the 3-hour break. I was in my element. I had classes of eager students ready to learn. I was doing presentations everywhere and anywhere to build exposure for this new program. I was going to fairs and conventions, associations and cafes, and doing everything I knew to make this program a success. The college had a booth at the 'Earth Day' Convention at Balboa Park. I showed up to work and boy did I ever. I was offering free Handwriting Analysis to everyone! I was doing their analysis on the spot and it took off! Everyone was stopping by, giving a handwriting sample, and waiting in line for me to give them their analysis. I did 120 handwriting analyses in a day! Yes, a personal best and still an unbroken record. It was phenomenal.

However, there was a downside to the whole Program Director experience. First, the people of the town I had moved to in the southernmost edge of San Diego shunned me. Nobody talked to me.

As I took my laundry down the pathway to the neighboring laundry room, people walking past me would turn their heads to look at the walk, instead of responding to my cordial 'good morning.'

I still cannot understand why it happened, but it did. Out of everyone in the complex, only one older gentleman would nod and respond with a smile.

Being alone became more significant when a stalker showed up at the college. He had driven 170 miles to come and apply for the course, because I was teaching it. The Admissions lady, too, felt that there was something wrong because of his outrageous comments about me. This was the only time in my life that I panicked. He had been a bother in the first college and had been escorted off the property. Then when he showed up in San Diego, I called the police. The officer who showed up was beyond supportive and caring, which is much more than I can say about the college and the Dean's response. Apart from the Dean being livid as to why the police were called, he emailed all the staff stating, "If anyone of you helps Maureen in this stalker situation she is dealing with, your job is on the line."

That meant that I was truly alone. I knew over the years that I had been alone, but I had never experienced this level of malice.

When there's a predator who is focused on you, the last thing you expect is for your own boss to ensure that you're a sitting duck – without any protection. I knew my friends would have liked to help me, but I understood that they couldn't risk their jobs.

61

I had to go to court for the restraining order, which meant I had to be in the same room with the stalker. Luckily, after questioning me with a soft voice, the brilliant judge hearing the case turned to him and went into 'lioness mode.' She was so strict and stern with him, that by the time she was done with him, he was sobbing. That was definitely a triumphant moment for me, especially because I had faced him alone.

That experience changed something in me. I had always known that I am courageous, but usually the courage was to help someone else! This time, my courage had been to aid myself! It was a new feeling, because due to my upbringing, I knew that I had had to speak up for me. For whatever reason, my parents were not the type of people who would confront authority regardless of the situation. So, it had been up to me to forge forward, many times. Yet, in all those scenarios, somewhere inside I had some level of safety. With this stalker, I had experienced real fear. He was mentally unstable, and I knew that there was no telling what he would do next.

His unpredictability is what scared me. He did not hold himself to our laws or to their consequences, so having to face it all alone was daunting. The lesson here is that I DID IT! Ironically, I can truly share with you how much stronger I have been since that experience.

I do not want any of you to live through something like that, but truth be told, I am stronger for having gone through it.

I had come to a decision. Taking everything into consideration, what was happening at the college, and the last straw – knowing that I did not have the backing or support from the Dean/Owner of the college, I resigned and returned to Los Angeles.

What would you have done in this situation? How have you reacted when your work environment turned sour? How did you speak up for yourself?

Chapter 10

This is when one of the most laborious chapters of my life began. I ran two offices – one in Los Angeles and one in San Diego - for six years. I lived half a week in one city and the other half in the other. The first four years, my home base was in Los Angeles, while the last two, it was in San Diego. I drove 400 miles a week. It was crazy! It was exhilarating! Both practices were thriving! Colleagues would ask me why I was doing this. Why was I doing this? The response I gave, and the truth was, "Because I can!"

I was helping two different groups of people and I loved every moment of it. I remembered being desperate on the couch begging God to give me a life. He sure had and I was not going to waste a moment of it!

Over the years, I have dealt with so many different types of people, so many different types of presenting complaints. For me, being a hypnotherapist is a vocation. I am beyond thankful that God blessed me with this career. Every day, I get to serve those who are ready to upgrade their life! I love asking 'How much better can life get?' and guess what... it does!

Here's a small sample of situations I've helped with.

- One man came in to stop smoking. He smoked 3 ½ packs a day! Can you imagine that? 70 cigarettes in a day? His motivator was his 16-year-old daughter asking him if he was going to be alive to walk her down the aisle. Thankfully, that was all the motivation he required. We did the smoking cessation session and he never picked up a cigarette again. That was over nine years ago.

Maureen A Pisani C.Ht., T.N.L.P
Maureenpisani.com

- I had a lady who had been raised well, but in an extremely sheltered environment. She expressed her desire to start dating. She was beautiful on the inside and out. She was eager to explore the world, but her parents' fear tactics to 'raise a good girl' were still resonating within her, even at this adult age. Slowly but surely, we worked through all the blocks, so she was able to start dating and have a relationship.

- I had a client a few years ago who was a professional through and through. He had been in practice for years and was known as a pillar in his community. There was only one problem, though. Every time he had to give a presentation or a training, he would break out in these horrible red blotches on his face. He knew his field, was an expert in it, but speaking in front of others made him extremely uncomfortable. He sought me out for a couple of sessions, and we readjusted how his unconscious mind identified these presentations. We removed that fight/flight trigger and got him to be comfortable and at ease everywhere he was.

- After a short while of listening to the recordings, he reached out to me to let me know that he could give presentations to large groups and still be completely at ease and confident, while his skin maintained a smooth, unblemished tone.

- I had another client who was beyond docile. She was as polite as they come. She was a true lady. Unfortunately, her husband was the opposite. He was loud, abrasive, and aggressive verbally and physically if the situation warranted it. She was mortified. She didn't know how to handle him in public or in private because he was beyond temperamental. We worked on solidifying her strength and her confidence. We worked on her having more words to express herself, integrated more behavioral patterns for assertiveness, and sometimes stipulated that walking away was enough of a pattern interrupt to shock him into snapping out of the aggressive attack mode and behaving appropriately. She found that hypnotherapy gave her the tools to strengthen her self-confidence, self-esteem, and self-worth.

- I worked with a lady, who, apart from being professional, was polite and polished. She was brilliant, elegant, and incredibly poised. She was a prim and proper married woman who was dealing with an incredibly difficult situation at work. She was the kind of lady who would not dare to hug someone unless they were a close friend or family member. She was as straight an arrow as they come, but here she was dealing with this scoundrel whose bad reputation was well known.

His behavior was outrageously inappropriate. Working with this lady hit many points for me. I was ready to help her as a therapist, and as a woman I wished her the ultimate of success. I knew we had to increase her levels of self-confidence, her assertiveness, and her self-worth. She pulled through. She made it happen! She had the courage to file the report, only to find out months later that subsequent to her reporting other ladies had come forward and corroborated her claims! This lady went through hell thinking she was alone, and as soon as she spoke up others echoed her report. It was remarkably interesting to see the change in this lady. Yes, she was prim and proper, but before our sessions she was also initially timid. As soon as she found out that there were many others, she found more strength in herself.

Maureen A Pisani C.Ht., T.N.L.P
Maureenpisani.com

She appreciated how much courage it took for her to speak out about her own situation, but then was incredibly grateful and proud that she had taken that step. That internal strength has resonated within her ever since. She advanced in her career and has also utilized all the tools and techniques we worked on in all the areas of her life.

- I had a young lady come to me with a question and a hopeful heart. She had this weird condition where 25% of her body would break out in blotches. There was no rhyme or reason. One appendage and a portion of her torso would be blotchy and blistered for a while, and eventually the skin would calm down. Then without warning, another appendage and adjoining torso section would flare up. Of course, I always want to give my best and help. Yes, we worked together for a couple of sessions. Yes, we discussed stress relieving techniques.

- Yes, we strategized on how to deal with her life situations. Even though I have an extensive medical background, I, too, found myself hoping that hypnotherapy would work for her sake. All she wanted was clear, smooth, unblemished skin - something you and I take for granted. I created personalized hypnotic recordings and off she went. Later in the year, I received a photo of her in a bikini at the beach! I was smiling for a whole week!

- I received a call from a cousin, from Malta, begging for my help. Her 16-year-old daughter needed a vaccine booster, but the girl was terrified of needles. Of course, I was going to help. My cousin took the phone to the daughter's room, where the teenager was literally on her bed sobbing. I asked her why she was crying, and her answer was "Because I'm going to die!" I remember chuckling softly. Just like a 16-year-old to catastrophize to that extent!

We worked together about why she needed the booster. I asked several questions and found out what she thought was 'ridiculous' and used it as a deflector.

69

I confirmed with her that it was ok with her to have a different reaction to needles. She was eager to feel better about needles. I proceeded to hypnotized her over FB messenger audio, and she was appropriately responsive. The three of us had agreed, that she, the daughter, was to listen to the recording as she fell asleep that night and as her mother, my cousin, was driving her to the doctor's office. I received a message the next day, expressing thanks and gratitude for an incredible outcome. Apparently, the 16-year-old started giggling and laughing out loud. She shared that the more her mind thought she should cry, the harder she laughed. It was a huge breakthrough for both! What was initially seen as a horrible experience turned into a hilarious memory.

- I worked with a client who had been the victim of mistaken identity. He was exiting a club in not too good of a neighborhood, when an entire gang attacked and beat him to a pulp. They were wearing steel-toed boots and they kicked him everywhere.

One of them had even dealt him that karate hit that pushed the nasal bone through the skull, in an attempt to kill him. Luckily, the skull had not fractured completely, and he survived.

However, he had had a constant level 9 pain, for over 20 years. When Botox was FDA approved, he was receiving 12 shots in the face every month, only to have the pain ease to a level 7. He came to see me as his last resort. After explaining how he experienced the pain, I hypnotized him. After 20 minutes in hypnosis, his pain level dropped to a level 2! From that moment onward, all this gentleman had to do was listen to the recording instead of popping another pill.

- I had a lady come in for a pre-surgical appointment. She had a horrible reaction to needles – she would just drop in a dead faint. She was scheduled to have a liposuction procedure done to her thighs and buttocks.

She was eager to get it done but was terrified because she knew how that procedure was done. Luckily, the surgeon was aware of the benefits of hypnotherapy. He had already agreed to have her listen to the hypnotic recording during the surgery. We worked together for a series of sessions, at the end of which she had a pre-surgery recording, a during-surgery recording, and a post-surgery recording.

I received a call the day after the procedure. She was ecstatic. She had listened to the pre-surgery recording as recommended and found that she was beyond relaxed as the day approached.

She had listened to the recording during the procedure. The cosmetic surgeon was concerned at how incredibly relaxed she was that he kept shaking her awake. She was particularly upset with him for interrupting her hypnotic journey. They were both aware that there was less bleeding, less swelling, less discomfort and faster healing with an increased level of comfort. Her healing rate was also faster than expected. Needless to say, my client was incredibly pleased with this outcome.

Maureen A Pisani C.Ht., T.N.L.P
Maureenpisani.com

- I also have had my share of sessions where the emotional pain the client was experiencing was excruciating. I received a call from a client asking if I had an availability that day. Her best friend had just lost her child and did not see any reason to continue living. Of course, I saw her ASAP. The client brought in her friend, who rightfully so, was beyond broken hearted. Now, years, later, I can admit that I too, was worried about this lady. She was experiencing possibly the most heartbreaking of situations. I had to buy time. In these situations,

I am incredibly grateful to God. Words, thoughts, plans came out of my mouth, that my ears heard for the first time. I am blessed and honored that the Almighty gifts me with His words.

I managed to get her to promise me that she would come in for three appointments. I knew that with three appointments I would have enough time to adjust things.

Maureen A Pisani C.Ht., T.N.L.P
Maureenpisani.com

Grief is an awful wound, especially when it's your child. It's not how the story should go. Your child should have a long and happy life, not this ending. We discussed everything – from life after death, to reincarnation, to energy, and to eternal unbreakable love between mother and child. She sobbed openly, allowing the pain to ooze out of her. I... cried at home. My heart broke for her. I was there to support and guide her through this storm. One session at a time, we met and worked... to release the pain, and to soothe the brain, the heart, and the mind. Slowly but surely her words started changing...and slowly, rays of sunshine began entering her world again. Will she ever get over her child's death? Of course not. But she has come to the point where she can live one day at a time, with the least amount of pain.

Maureen A Pisani C.Ht., T.N.L.P
Maureenpisani.com

- I had a client who lost her Dad in a car crash. It was so sudden he was gone instantaneously. There was no closure. She missed him terribly. She had wanted to share so many things, but he was gone. Even though her brain logically understood it, her mind and her heart struggled terribly. We worked together and I implemented a technique dear to my heart, because I know how effective it is. I got her to receive a visit from her Dad while in Hypnosis. She saw him, she hugged him, she felt his arms hugging her, and she felt him kissing her forehead. She sat down with him and talked to him – heart to heart. I helped ease certain things that I knew needed to be smoothened out. She had a long enough time with him to soothe that initial surprise. I ended it in a way that soothed her heart, knowing and confirming that this was not the only time that she was to spend time with him and that he would return. As soon as I brought her out of the hypnotic state, I shared with her that I had recorded the session for her so she could listen to it any time her heart desired. She was overjoyed. This technique keeps soothing hearts all around the world.

- I have also had clients who come seeking deep understandings to questions they cannot ask anyone else.

After an abusive parent dies, all they feel is relief, and they feel that that's an inappropriate reaction. Our sessions cover self-love, self-acceptance, self-forgiveness, and many other aspects of how to deal with this delicate situation. We are raised to believe that parents should be loving, caring, and protective. However, when that does not happen, outsiders who are not privy to what happened within the family dynamics expect the family to mourn. That's what the British call a 'sticky wicket.' It's an incredibly delicate situation that's different for each person. My role in their life, as their therapist, is to guide them through acceptance of what the reality was, releasing it, and seeing how they can move on from here, where each day is lived with intention, respect, and love – even if just to themselves. In my humble opinion, they have been through enough.

Maureen A Pisani C.Ht., T.N.L.P
Maureenpisani.com

From this point forward, they need to be appreciated, cared for, accepted, and loved. It's so new that initially they do not even recognize it as a good thing. Eventually, as time goes by, hindsight increases understandings, which enhances the depth of gratitude they feel.

- Then, there are the clients who have been treated horribly in a relationship. I have had both men and women, seeking solace, peace, and understanding after a narcissist wreaked havoc in their life. Narcissists are what I consider the 'plague' in today's world. These ego-centric monsters manipulate, coerce, gaslight, abuse, twist the truth, lie through their teeth, and steam roll right over the people they have in their lives, especially the ones they profess to love. These evil Machiavellian usurpers have no conscience and will stomp right over the one they claim to love if there's a possibility for them to get more attention, more praise, more 'spotlight.' Their life is all about them, always. When clients come to me, after having gone through that kind of hell, they're broken and fragile.

77

They simply cannot trust anyone because what if they end up trusting in another narcissist? Remember, narcissists will present as charming, loving, and wonderful, while in reality, they are the exact opposite. Working with these incredibly honest, truthful, loving yet fragile clients makes my day. My contribution to their lives is that we get to upgrade their minds and thinking patterns to set healthy, strong boundaries that make them resolute. We get to launch a new future, where each has a strong sense of self-love, self-confidence, self-esteem, and self-worth.

The process is as slow or as fast as the client's mind can handle. I gift the personalized recording to the client specifically for that reason… to allow the client to determine their own pace. Listening to the recording as they fall asleep ensures that suggestions are reinforced, and upgrades are permanently set.

Maureen A Pisani C.Ht., T.N.L.P
Maureenpisani.com

Chapter 11

It was 2011, when I received a call from the Medical Director of the Chopra Center. A guest had recommended having me there as a speaker. The Director set up an appointment for an interview. After a 2 ½ hour interview, I looked around her office and casually stated that I would require less than half of her office to see the guests. She had only thought of me as an occasional speaker, but I had other plans. I explained to her that if she wanted me to really help the center's guests, then offering hypnotherapy as a regular service would be appropriate.

I started giving presentations to their Perfect Health Groups and soon ended up being sold out for every Perfect Health Cycle. What initially was planned as an occasional gig, thanks to my 'creative thinking' turned me into their #1 seller! I was the Resident Hypnotherapist at the Chopra Center for 8 ½ years, till its closure in December 2019. Yes, I was pleased. Yes, I worked hard. Yes, I thrived. It was phenomenal for me to be working with guests who were open-minded and eager to receive the tools and upgrade their lives.

I was also still running my private practice and I was still learning. My belief is that for me to serve at my best, I must study. The Hypnotherapy world, unfortunately, is an unregulated industry, so dilettantes who take a 4-week training think they can go out there and change the world.

At this point, I've been in practice for 15 years and haven't stopped studying. Most practitioners take the basic levels of training in a couple of modalities and tandem them in their practice. I am at the master's Level in all 5 – Hypnosis, Therapeutic Guided Imagery, Neuro-Linguistic Programming, Emotional Freedom Technique, and Reiki. I'm also the only hypnotherapist who has been a Director and Instructor in two nationally accredited colleges, not to mention that I am co-author on a research paper published through the Neuro-Science Department at U.C.L.A.

There is one thing I know for sure: I will continue learning and studying and honing my skills so I can continuously serve my clients with the best I have to offer.

What opportunities have you seized? What opportunities have you created? How have you looked at possibilities? What's your mindset? Are you open to receive new opportunities?

Chapter 12

As I think back, I remember the moment I realized that every single experience that I had lived was what I have now termed "Front-row research." You know that saying – *'Things happen for a reason,'* right? Well, there's a second part to that saying… and it is *'And that reason is there to serve you.'*

Hindsight, as wise and as valuable as it is, gifted me the awareness that I was truly born to be a hypnotherapist. However, because of realistic logistics I had gone down the only pathway that was available to me. I could only have chosen to be trained in the Western medical system, because that's all that was available to me back then. I would have continued down that pathway, if God had not intervened with a great big wallop to the side of my head!

Of course, figuratively speaking! He got me at the elbows!

Considering who I am, and everything I've been through, I needed to be jolted out of my day-to-day life for me to be open to new possibilities. Subtle hints had not worked, so, something cataclysmic had to happen in my life for me to stop and search for new ways of living, of thinking, of being.

Maureen A Pisani C.Ht., T.N.L.P
Maureenpisani.com

What I expected to be a disadvantage, my accent, ended up being an asset in my practice. Hypnosis is known to come from a 'far-away-land,' and the accent just confirms that I, too, come from a far-away-land. Ironically, it tends to add credence to what I do.

All those chapters, taking me down so many different routes, are now thoroughly appreciated. I now acknowledge them as building my 'library' to be able to understand, accept, guide, teach, and help more people. I have a deeper understanding of life. I tend to find that looking at the big picture really prevents me from saying or doing anything rash.

As a professional therapist and a mentor, I hold myself to higher standards.

Over the decades I have seen many lose their composure. I have always wondered why they didn't simply choose to pause. Learning and implementing a 'pause' has saved me from many an uncomfortable situation. I believe in that saying - 'you cannot *un-ring* a bell.' There are many who blurt out things in a moment of anger, only to be riddled with guilt and regret afterward. Instilling that 'pause' would have bought that individual enough time to take a breath, calm down, gather their wits, and then speak... with intention. This strategy would save a lot of relationships and prevent many a broken heart.

Maureen A Pisani C.Ht., T.N.L.P
Maureenpisani.com

When I think about how I dealt with people – all kinds of people – family, loved ones, friends, colleagues, clients, students, even strangers, I know I came from a good place in my heart. Very rarely have I ever said things out of anger. Remember, I know we are each responsible for our actions. Nobody is going to make me do something I don't want to do. I do it, because I determine that it's the right move for me, the right statement, the right action, or the right decision.

In 30 years of adulthood while in relationships, I have raised my voice five times. Yes, I remember those incidents.

I had to raise my voice, because the person I was dealing with was ignoring what I was saying at a lower volume.

In fact, truth be told, nothing is ever a wasted effort. When we think about our past, we remember who we helped, how they responded, and how good it felt when they were grateful. However, I know you remember when you helped someone and they turned on you, don't you? Just like you, I do too. I know I am generous, especially if I know that someone needs a helping hand. I've helped countless people, yet a few, sporadically, snap at me with a surprising level of ingratitude that shocks me. Again, remember, I know I am responsible for my actions. So, it's up to me how I respond.

Maureen A Pisani C.Ht., T.N.L.P
Maureenpisani.com

Considering that after everything I've done for them, they are so ungrateful, the first decision for me is to stop helping. There are others I can help who would at least show some gratitude. The second decision, usually after I see how they react once they realize that I've stopped helping them – which is usually even more negative - is to stop communicating with them. For whatever reason, they decided to be aggressive in a scenario where that was the worst response possible.

If you notice, I haven't done anything against them. I just removed myself from that equation. Once I learn their true colors, I know where I stand with those people and according to what that outcome is, I make my decisions. I don't hold any animosity towards them. I just go on with my life.

There's a saying 'Where you go, you will follow,' meaning those individuals because of their behavior will keep creating similar scenarios. If the identity that they feel suits them is a negative one, they will self-sabotage and twist good things around, so their usual ending occurs, and they once again confirm that *that* is who they are!

Every situation is a learning opportunity. It's either teaching me what I need to do, or what I should never do again. I choose to remain open to the learning.

Maureen A Pisani C.Ht., T.N.L.P
Maureenpisani.com

Everyone is capable of making their own decisions, of responding to different scenarios in different ways. All I do is watch, observe, and assess what I need to absorb from this particular event, and then be proactive in my decisions and actions.

Being Catholic, I know that at some point I will be coming face-to-face with God. I will be judged on MY decisions and actions, according to what my INTENTION was at the time. The same public action could be good or bad.

It all depends on the internal intention that caused that action. Only you and God know what that truth is. So be aware of your intentions.

Chapter 13

Our lives are like pyramids, they're built on a foundation and layer after layer, we keep building until we reach our pinnacle.

The strength of the pyramid – the success of our life - depends on the foundation. Knowing what comprises the foundation is essential for a fulfilling life. The foundation is our Self-Identity, which is a combination of Self-Confidence, Self-Esteem, Self-Worth, Self-Acceptance, Self-Respect and Self-Love. If one of these is not at its highest of levels, the pyramid will be lopsided.

As you can imagine, every negative event in our lives chips away at these six foundational core requirements so most of us don't have strong levels.

However, all are essential for a thriving future. If one has low Self-Worth, then they won't have the drive to go out there and strive for a better tomorrow, right? If one has low Self-Respect, can you see how that would affect what decisions they make? If one has low Self-Acceptance, they will be their worst enemy. If one has low Self-Esteem, they won't think they deserve better. If one has low Self-Confidence, they won't believe they can do whatever they are hoping to achieve. If one has low Self-Love, then all kinds of self-destructive behaviors will occur in life.

Each of us thinks we're doing ok until a crisis occurs. If everything is calm, peaceful, and happy, we never think we need to upgrade. However, when something tips the balance, that's when we realize something's not functioning at the peak of its efficiency. People usually don't realize that how they were living was deficient until they experience better.

Most have tons of excuses why their significant other treats them the way they do, because internally they feel that that's all they deserve. Most die a thousand deaths before asking for a raise, because they don't feel they're worthy of it.

Maureen A Pisani C.Ht., T.N.L.P
Maureenpisani.com

Most do not apply for their dream job, because they don't think they can get it. Most self-sabotage their health with intentionally chosen wrong foods because they have a very low opinion of themselves. Most won't invest in themselves because they don't think they could succeed.

If you had to take a look at how 'healthy' your self-identity is, what will you find? How strong are your Self-Confidence, Self-Esteem, Self-Worth, Self-Acceptance, Self-Respect and Self-Love? Which needs a little (or a big) boost?

As I went through all these chapters in life, I found that I had to face each and every one of these aspects of myself.

Because I hadn't been taught to value them (it wasn't a thing back then), I was living life crossing my fingers and hoping for the best, so to speak.

Drastic and dramatic situations happened to me because I would not have learned to step up for myself otherwise. If the insult was minor or subtle, I would have ignored it.

However, for me to have a great day-to-day existence, leading to a great future, I had to raise those standards. So, situations arose in my life where I had to take a stand and speak up for myself. That's the best irony of all. What I initially saw as 'bad' experiences were simply life lessons – opportunities for Self-Improvement! All of 'them' had to behave so outrageously bad, so I could see them for who they truly were. Their negative behavior was so blatant that it pushed me past what I thought of as being compassionate and understanding and landed me solidly in the reality of the matter. This way, I could confidently state 'Enough is enough!' and walk away. Lines had to be crossed for me to take a stand, for me to speak up, and for me to eventually realize how much strength I had, because I *had* said 'NO.'

Here's how my own levels increased or decreased in the before mentioned situations.

EVENT	S.C.	S.E.	S.W.	S.A.	S.R.	S.L.
Easter Sunday Event – Saving Dad's Life	+		+			
Grandma's comment	-		-			-
Being Shy during high school	-	-	-	-	-	-
Stressed out with Organic Chemistry	-	-	-	-	-	-

Maureen A Pisani C.Ht., T.N.L.P
Maureenpisani.com

Deciding on appendectomy	+	+	+	+	+	+
Defying the neurosurgeon	+		+		+	
Dealing with infertility	-	-	-	-	-	-
End of first marriage – Accepting Freedom	+	+	+	+	+	+
Injured Arms Episode	-	-	-	-	-	-
Left Arm Blisters Experience	+	+	+	+	+	+
Being Titled 100% Disabled	-	-	-	-	-	-

Getting mad about being called 100% disabled	+	+	+	+	+	+
Beginning Hypnotherapy Course	+	+	+	+	+	+
Impromptu Giving Demo in Class	+	+	+	+	+	+
End of second marriage – Accepting Freedom	+	+	+	+	+	+

89

	S.C.	S.E.	S.W.	S.A.	S.R.	S.L.
The effect of being yelled at, at work	+	+	+	+	+	+
Realizing stalker found me	-					
Winning court case against stalker	+	+	+	+	+	+
Running 2 offices in 2 different cities	+	+	+	+	+	+
Chopra Center Interview	+	+	+	+	+	+
Becoming #1 Seller at Chopra Center	+	+	+	+	+	+

- S.C. – Self-Confidence
- S.E. – Self-Esteem
- S.W. – Self-Worth
- S.A. – Self-Acceptance
- S.R. – Self-Respect
- S.L. – Self-Love

As you can see, I look at life events in a different manner than most. Yes, there are situations that are just seen as bad – my grandmother's comment being one of them.

Maureen A Pisani C.Ht., T.N.L.P
Maureenpisani.com

However, even in that situation, I shared that that comment triggered me to become addicted to studying! How you catalog the event in your conscious and eventually in your unconscious mind will have a resultant effect on how you live your life. I have looked at the ending of a marriage as accepting freedom. I look for and usually find *hidden blessings* in every situation I face.

When I helped save my Dad's life, that increased levels of Self-Confidence because I knew that if I could do *that,* I could do anything! Being shy in high school and having those blisters in college lowered all of the Self-Identity levels. I was functioning from a space of being 'less-than.'

However, when I made the decision to have the elective appendectomy, I was able to make that decision because my Self-Identity levels were all high and solid. Facing infertility crushed all my levels.

However, ironically, the ending of the first marriage boosted all those levels, because I knew I deserved a man who would truly be there for me. Getting hurt on the job and going through that entire sequence of unfortunate events with the elbow surgeries, crushed all my levels of Self-Identity again. However, even though levels were so low, I still had the ability to stand up for myself when necessary.

91

Remember, when I shared the experience of having those blisters on the left elbow and I had to fight the surgeon to be seen and treated appropriately?

Well, today I see that as me standing up, speaking up for myself, because I knew I deserved better treatment.

When they declared me 100% disabled, didn't I have the perfect opportunity to live my life under the label of 'victim?' However, thanks to my solid level of Self-Esteem (knowing I do deserve better), I spoke up and fought against that label and thankfully was blessed with a second future. When I was asked to do the demo in class, I had never done any hypnotherapy in public. However, because of my studies I knew I could do it. Because of a high level of Self-Confidence, I succeeded in doing the demo that launched my teaching career. When the second marriage ended, it ended because deep down in my heart I knew I deserved better. Today, I can share that a healthy Self-Esteem liberated me!

When the other instructor was yelling at me, internally a part of me was thinking 'Wow! I really had to have done something impressive for him to get SO INCREDIBLY upset!' Plus, he ended up giving me the BEST label EVER! When life hit me between the eyes with the stalker situation, I experienced real fear. However, the definition of courage is 'being afraid and doing it anyway.'

Maureen A Pisani C.Ht., T.N.L.P
Maureenpisani.com

I HAD to face him because I knew I deserved true peace of mind. I had to handle it and I did. It helped me realize the intense inner strength I own and of course, raised all the levels. When I ran two offices in two different cities, it was definitely a lot of work, but those six years reinforced that I can set *and* achieve all of my goals!

See what I mean? Sometimes phenomenal presents show up in ugly wrapping. Taking a moment to go past the wrapping transforms our understanding, acceptance, and appreciation of the present.

Now I live every day from a humble space in life, incredibly grateful that God has gifted me with such a journey. Are there times when it feels daunting? Absolutely. Are there times it's difficult? Yes. However, I know that with my faith in God, His blessings, my techniques and practice, my brain, my mind, my intentions, and my love, I know I'm on the right path.

These understandings emerged after I had delved into this mesmerizing world of alternative complementary medicine.

Hypnotherapy is probably the most misunderstood modality. Between the myths and misconceptions that have survived over the centuries, most who have heard the word 'hypnosis' only think of stage hypnosis and all the shenanigans that occur on stage.

93

Hypnotherapy is hypnosis utilized for therapeutic purposes only... quite different than what goes on in the stage hypnosis scenarios.

However, the secret as to why hypnotherapy has been transforming lives for centuries is because through hypnosis, one can access the unconscious mind. That's the missing piece for many modalities.

When we go for 'talk-therapy,' all we're engaging is our conscious mind, which is only 12% of our brain power. Hypnotherapy gets the other 88% involved.

The conscious mind is incredibly capable of creating new goals, dreams and wishes. However, that's all it can do... create them. The ability to achieve those goals is completely dependent on whether your unconscious mind is in alignment or not. The programming that's running in the unconscious mind is usually set by age 8.

But I have a feeling that your current dreams, wishes, and goals differ slightly than the ones you had as a child. Truth be told, regardless of what your conscious mind's wishes are, the unconscious mind determines what happens in your todays and your tomorrows.

So, unless the unconscious mind's programming is updated, you will be stuck in the old thinking, the old levels of achievement and the old abilities to earn what you thought was appropriate when you were 8 years of age. Once hypnotherapy is in your life, you can literally tailor what you want to achieve. And once 100% of your brain power is involved, then all those goals, dreams, and wishes are achieved with surprising ease.

I joke with clients that working with me is like _me going to the gym, and you getting the six-pack!_ I've done the studies and have the understandings, and with the magnificent tool of hypnotherapy, our mental collaboration results in your having upgrades that become intrinsic to who you are, leading you to a phenomenal future.

When one has these kinds of interactions, it's difficult not to desire more! Over the years, people have attempted to chastise me for being a workaholic, but to me this is not work. This is being of service. This is bringing hope, happiness, and love to people's lives. I am living a vocation, where I cherish the fact that the message that I send out from my heart, that I am here for you, is received. I have had clients from years past reach out to me because something happened, and the only person they could think to discuss it with was me. That's an incredible honor for me.

Maureen A Pisani C.Ht., T.N.L.P
Maureenpisani.com

As I reach the conclusion of this book, I would like you to think about your past, only to see:

(i)   how far you've come
(ii) what events can you now re-label as learning opportunities, and
(iii) how much stronger, wiser and amazing you are!

Keep in mind that just because we now have these levels of awareness doesn't mean that life is just going to be a walk in the park. Our soul needs more lessons, so yes, we will probably face some stormy waters, but now we know we're strong sailors in the seas of life. Now, we know we can handle whatever comes our way.

Now, we know that every event is an opportunity to learn, to live, and to love!

With these new tools, we, each of us can voluntarily upgrade ourselves from just merely existing to truly thriving!

May God continue to bless you all!

Maureen A Pisani C.Ht., T.N.L.P
Maureenpisani.com

Biography

As an Author and Motivational Speaker, Maureen utilizes her experiences to highlight how each of us has hidden strengths within us.

As a Hypnotherapist, Maureen is at the Mastery Level in all five modalities – Hypnotherapy, Therapeutic Guided Imagery, Neuro-Linguistic Programming (NLP), Emotional Freedom Technique (E.F.T.) and Reiki Energy work. In addition, she is the ONLY Hypnotherapist who has been a Director and Instructor in two Nationally Accredited Colleges and is also a Trainer for NLP. Because of her medical and scientific training and background, she is also the ONLY Hypnotherapist who is a co-author of a research paper issued by the Neuroscience Department at UCLA. She was the resident Hypnotherapist at the renowned Chopra Center in La Costa, San Diego County, CA until its closure in December 2019.

Maureen has authored 12 books and produced more than 25 Hypnotic CDs. All of these products are available on her websites - www.prothrivesbh.com or www.maureenpisani.com

She is the founder of Pro-Thrive Science-Based Hypnotherapy, where she works with groups and individuals, in person or online, to help them go from just surviving to truly thriving.

Other books by author

- **Invisible to Invincible**
- **'Timeless Hypnotic Scripts I'**
- **'Timeless Hypnotic Scripts II'**
- **Conquering Covid-19**
  - Hypnotherapy & EFT Workbook with 1 Hypnotic MP3
- **Conquering Crisis**
  - Hypnotherapy & EFT Workbook with 1 Hypnotic MP3
- **3 Easy Steps to achieve *SUCCESS***
  - Hypnotherapy & EFT Workbook with 3 Hypnotic MP3s
- **3 Easy Steps for *Relationships***
  - Hypnotherapy & EFT Workbook with 3 Hypnotic MP3s
- **3 Easy Steps for *Weight Management***
  - Hypnotherapy & EFT Workbook with 3 Hypnotic MP3s
- **3 Easy Steps for a successful '*Hypnotherapy Practice*'**
  - Hypnotherapy & EFT Workbook with 3 Hypnotic MP3s

Maureen A Pisani C.Ht., T.N.L.P
Maureenpisani.com

- **3 Easy Steps for *Resilience***
  - Hypnotherapy & EFT Workbook with 1 Hypnotic MP3

- **Living a Pain & Medication Free Life**
  - Hypnotherapy & EFT Workbook with 1 Hypnotic MP3
- **R.I.D. Relieving Intestinal Discomfort**
  - Hypnotherapy & EFT Workbook with 1 Hypnotic MP3
- **'401 Study Guide'**
  - Supplementary Textbook to HMI 401 Course
- **Getting Away with it**
  - A fictional romance

Maureen A Pisani C.Ht., T.N.L.P
Maureenpisani.com